Learn Korean in a Day

A Silly Story Will Help It Stay!

Marcy Schaaf

It all started with me pointing a
gun (ㄱ),
That makes a sound like "guh."
What fun!

Next, I smelled something with my
nose (‿).
That's the sound of "n," so now
it' s known!

I opened the door (⊏), making a
"d" sound.
What do I see? A surprise is
inbound!

A rattlesnake (ㄹ) was right in
my way,
The sound is "r" or "l," that's
what I say!

My mouth (口) opened wide, ready
to shout.
"Mmm" is the sound that comes
right out!

I grabbed a bucket (ב), hoping
to catch,
A "b" sound, but I missed my
match!

The snake slithered fast, so I ran up the summit (ㅅ). The sound is "s," where the mountain hits it!

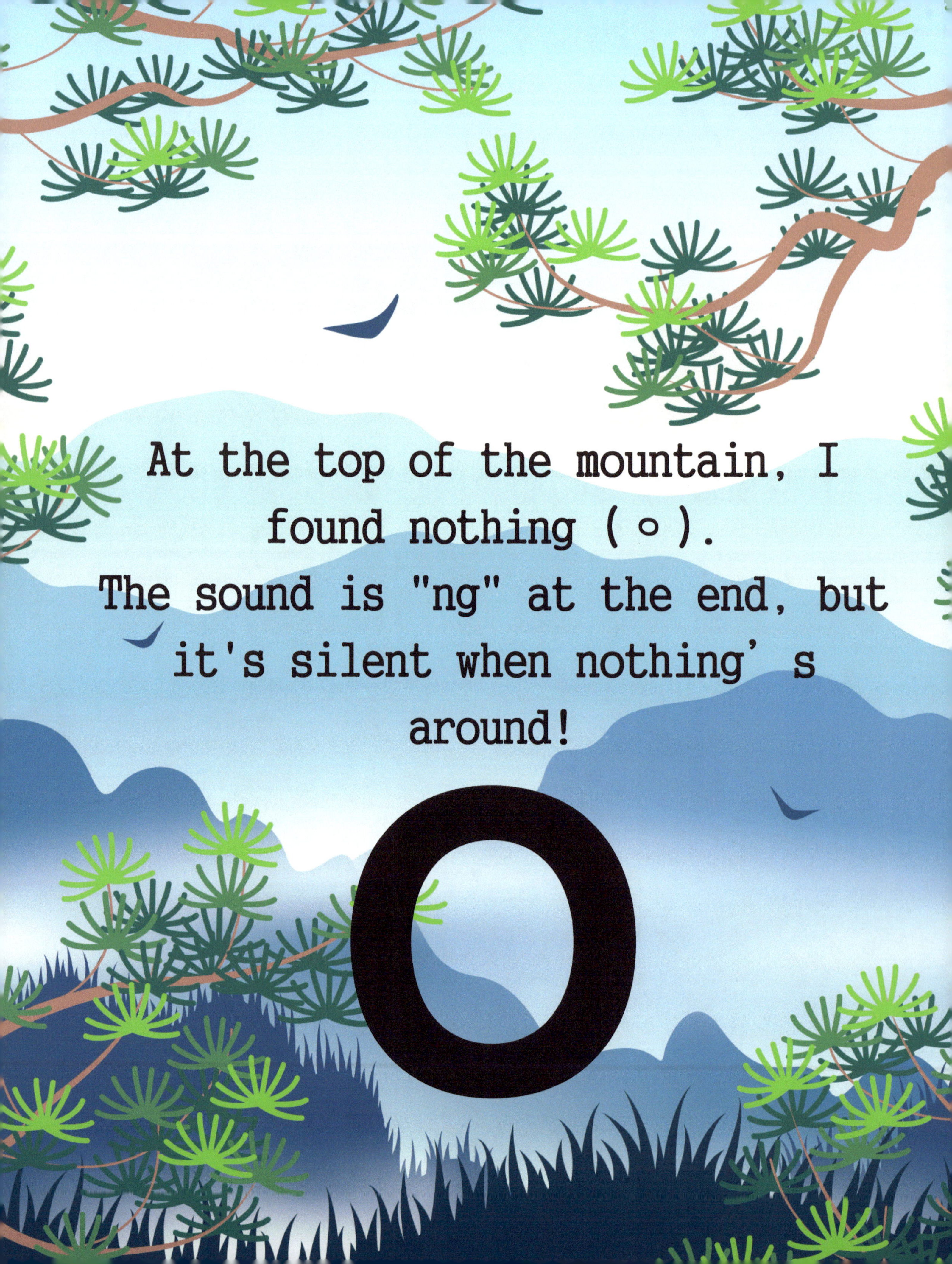At the top of the mountain, I found nothing (○).
The sound is "ng" at the end, but it's silent when nothing' s around!
O

In frustration, I decided to jump
(ㅈ).
With a "j" sound, I was in a big
slump!

But then I became a champion
(ㅊ), oh so bold,
"Ch" is the sound—I'm brave and
controlled!

I had new courage, I wanted to
kill (ㄱ) the snake,
"K" is the sound, but what a
mistake!

I missed the snake and hit the door (⊏).
The door split in two (⫤) with a loud "t" roar!

I'm not giving up, I'll push
down pillars (ㅍ).
"P" is the sound, I'll bring
down the thrillers!

But then, out of nowhere, a man
with a hat (ㅎ) appeared.
"H" is the sound, and the mystery
man cheered!

"Wait a minute!" the mystery man said.
"You just learned all the Korean consonants in your head!"

"Now let's learn vowels—let's
make it clear.
The symbol for 'ee' is like a
tree, straight and near."

"Put the man with the hat (ㅎ) in front of the tree,
Now you have the word 'He (히).' See how easy that can be?"

히 = He

"If the ʻeeʼ tree symbol leans
in too close,"
"It makes an ʻuhh (ㅡ)ʼ sound,
like something gross!"

"When the tree stretches away, it feels just right.
The sound is ‘ahh (ㅏ),’ like relaxing in the sunlight."

"Let's put these sounds together
and make a word.
With 'b (ㅂ),' 'ahh (ㅏ),'
'n (ㄴ),' you get ban (반)-
that's absurd!"

B + ahh+ n

"Now let's stretch it out and
make it twice as fun.
Add another 'ahh' and 'n' —
look, you've got banana (바나
나)! We're almost done."

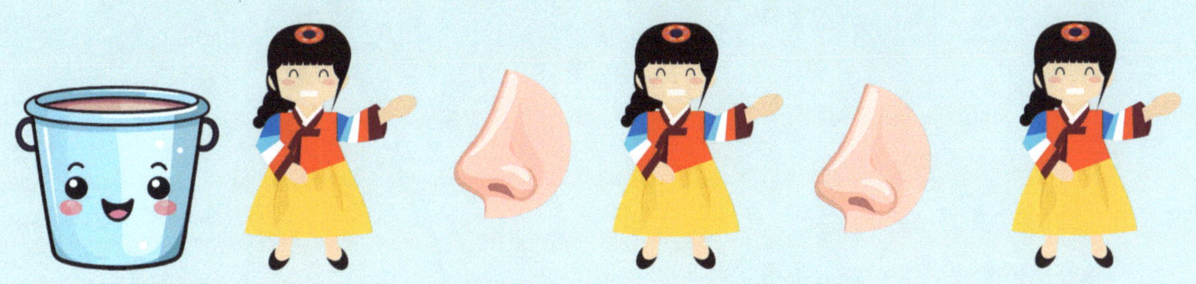

B + a + n + a + n + a

"Congratulations! You're learning fast,
You've unlocked the basics—this will last!"

"Now go ahead and explore more words,
Each consonant and vowel flies like birds."

"So if you see a gun (ㄱ), say
'guh' with pride,
Or open a door (ㄷ) to see what's
inside."

"Remember that nose (‿) makes
the sound 'n,'
And don't forget the
rattlesnake (ᵌ) again!"

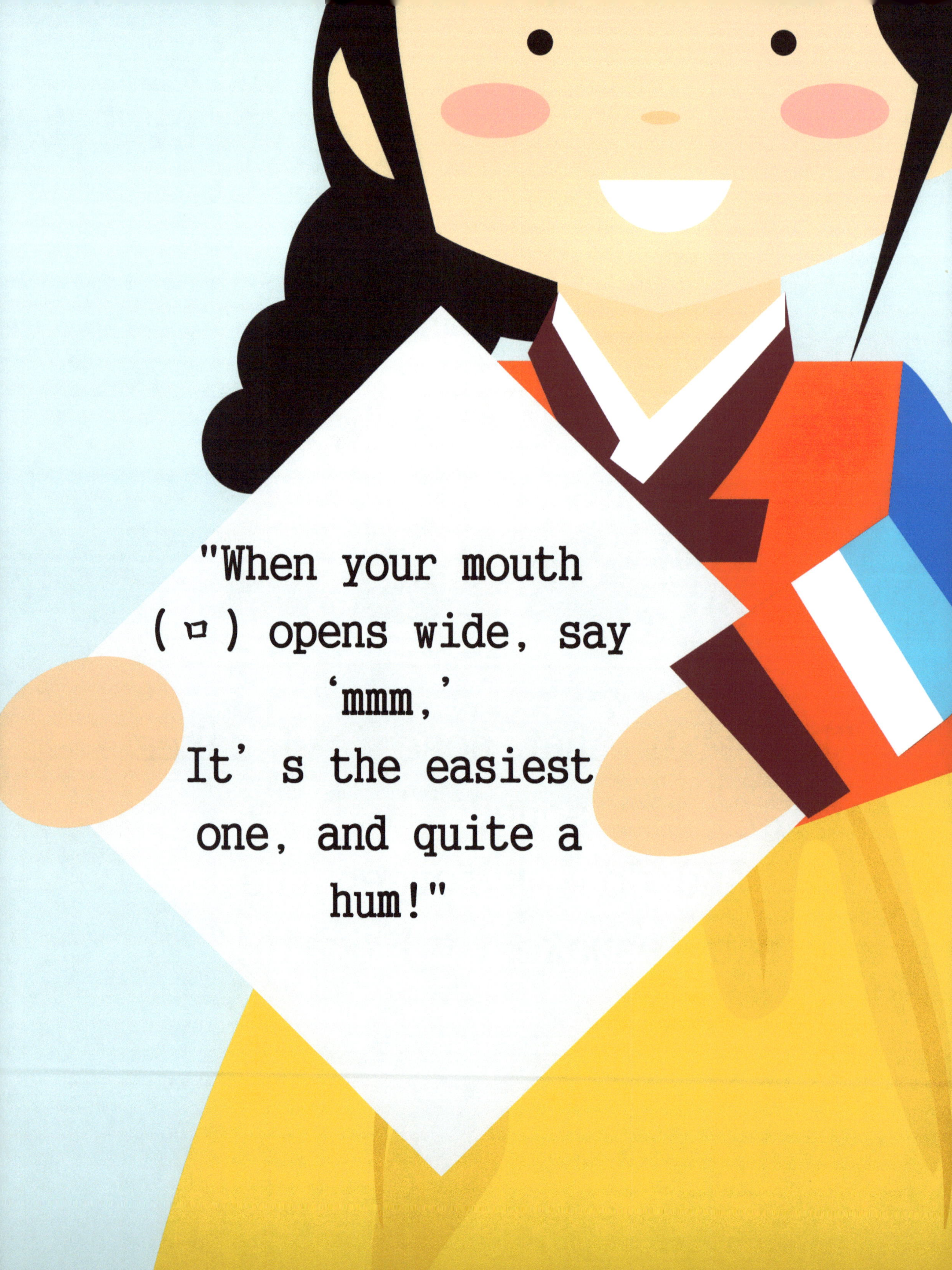

"When your mouth
(ㅁ) opens wide, say
'mmm,'
It's the easiest
one, and quite a
hum!"

"Try catching
things with your
bucket (ㅂ) that
goes 'b,'
And the summit
(ㅅ) at the top
makes the sound
's,' so
easily."

"If you find nothing (○), it's silent—just a space,
But when it's at the end, 'ng' is its place."

"Make a jump (ㅈ) when you see a
hill,
And be a champion (ㅊ) with all
your skill."

"Kill (ㅋ) your fears with a
'k' sound snap,
And break things in two (ㅌ) with
a 't' sound clap."

"Push the pillars (ㅍ) with a
powerful 'p,'
And tip your hat (ㅎ), because
now you' re free!"

"So now, let's
practice what
we've learned
today,
It's a silly
adventure, but you
found the way!"

"Start with b (ㅂ)
and ahh (ㅏ), then
say it slow,
Add n (ㄴ) and
more ahh (ㅏ)-
there you go!"

"Don't be afraid if things seem new,
You can learn Korean—yes, it's true!"

"Now let's explore vowels and
sounds even more,
The world of Korean has so much
in store."

"From the gun (ㄱ) to the hat (ㅎ), you've learned the basics, You're ready to practice, so let's not forsake it!"

"The more you read, the more you'll see,
Korean is fun—just like climbing a tree!"

"So give yourself
a cheer, a happy
jump (ㅈ) and say,
I've learned all
14 consonants
today—hip, hip,
hooray!"

"So give yourself a
cheer, a happy jump (ㅈ)
and say,
I've learned all 14
consonants today—hip,
hip, hooray!"

Books By Schaaf

www.BookBySchaaf.com

Find us at: